To Mom
Love Jenell & Scott
Aug. 18, 1992

Where Feelings Flower

Where Feelings Flower

POETRY OF LDS WOMEN

COLLECTED BY BARBARA B. SMITH & SHIRLEY W. THOMAS

BOOKCRAFT

SALT LAKE CITY, UTAH

Poems on pages 4, 6, 10 (top), 12, 16, 20, 22, 23, 34, 44, 45, 46, 48, 50, 55, 56, 57, 58, 62, 64, 66, 76, 90, 93, 105, 121, 144, and 160 (bottom) were first published in the Ensign *magazine and are used by permission.*

Library of Congress Catalog Card Number: 91–77871
ISBN 0–88494–821–8

First Printing, 1992

Printed in the United States of America

Contents

Contents

Contents

Contents

———— Gratitude for Growing Old ————

Introduction

The writing of poetry among Latter-day Saint women had its archetype in Eliza R. Snow, whose lively mind and ready pen earned her the affectionate title of "Zion's poetess." Her writings, always generous and fitting, and sometimes profound, were prized by early Latter-day Saints. Even more, they seemed to establish an expectation and clearly an appreciation of poetic composition among Mormon women. Today writers in the Church are numerous; women of the Church often use verse to express feelings growing out of their faith. In this book we have tried to capture the spirit of these women as it is found in their writings.

All of them write out of a common Latter-day Saint context—though with widely varying training and definite differences in style and technique. They write of their longing and fears, their strivings and love; they describe their homes and the world around them; but woven into this variety of subject matter is a common thread—a security of feeling that belief in God can bring. In that shared faith, these Latter-day Saint women speak to the heart, where essential belief and meaning are found.

Like other fashions over the years, styles in meter and rhyme have changed since the days of Eliza R. Snow. No longer are poems as didactic in tone or as measured in form as they once were. Yet, to make this collection somewhat representative in scope, we have included several of Sister Snow's poems as well as others that were written in her time and somewhat later. Although these older poems may seem a bit quaint, there remains in them a power that comes through the dated meter and diction.

Largely, however, the poems in this book are the works of contemporary women. Some are professional authors, and published volumes of their writings attest to the merit of their work. Other women whose work is included wrote as time allowed. But if many of their poems were written at the kitchen table, they are not, as William Butler Yeats describes, "the bundle of accident and incoherence that sits down to breakfast." Rather, the pieces are usually thoughtful, often include interesting insights, and frequently sparkle with surprising delight and wisdom.

The selections in this book could not, of course, include works by all writers of poetry among Mormon women. Furthermore, the pieces that have been included may not be representative of all that the selected authors have written. Taken together, however, these poems become an expression of a unique spirit, a voice of strength, a reinforcement of faith. "Whatsoever things are lovely, whatsoever things are of good report; if there be any virtue, and if there be any praise, think on these things" (Philippians 4:8).

Affinity
for the
Earth

"The earth is full of the goodness of the Lord"
—Psalm 33:5

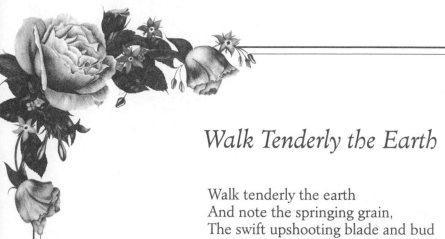

Walk Tenderly the Earth

Walk tenderly the earth
And note the springing grain,
The swift upshooting blade and bud
Where lately snow has lain.
The shine of new green leaves
Upon the bended limb.
Walk tenderly the earth
　　Remembering him.

Walk tenderly the earth
In blackened loam or sand,
On gentle slope or steepest crag,
Or on the moist, rich land.
Within the bright of morning
Or in the evening dim,
Walk tenderly the earth
　　Remembering him.

Walk tenderly the earth
And hear her choirs sing,
The silent symphonies of stars,
And meadows antheming.
Along a wooded violet stream
Or sudden canyon's rim,
Join tenderly the earth
　　In praising him.

—Helen M. Livingston

Having Risen

Unnumbered
shades of green
greet me in my garden.

He who planted Eden
chose them one by one,
including some only bees can see.

I will know His hands
(if I should see them),
not just from the wounds,
but from the callous places.

Who sends the rain and seeds,
and leaf and tree,
sends me.

Mary was right the first time, too
that morning
having arrived at the open tomb.
He is The Gardener.

—Margary B. Broadbent

Quiet Loveliness

The loveliest of earthly things
Move softly as the gauzy wings
Of brilliant springtime butterflies.
You cannot hear an opening rose,
Nor catch the sound of grass that grows;
In silence white clouds rise.

The rainbow stretches, proud and tall;
Leaves change to scarlet in the fall
In quietness at nature's nod.
The stars, the moon, the sunlight, too,
Send a soundless message through:
"Be still, and know that I am God."

—Grace Barker Wilson

Weeds

Weeds have a beauty all their own,
Though we leave them quite alone.
Along the ditchbank or against the fence,
Weeds are arrayed with diffidence.
Wind-tossed, shaking, mud-mixed and bent—
Still, yes—still they are heaven sent.

—Ida Isaacson

Whisperings of Spring

Snow was everywhere
And everywhere
Was silence

Until the sun spoke
Of the whisperings
Of spring.

The softened snow
Trickled onto the
Still-frozen stream
And the silence melted.

Darkness was everywhere
And everywhere
Was silence

Until the Son spoke
Of the whisperings
Of hope.

The Savior's love
Distilled onto the
Garden where He knelt
And the silence gave way to spring.

—Charlotte Anne Hutchins

The Year the Yuccas Bloomed

This is the year
The yuccas bloomed—
Each sturdy shaft
Stood proudly plumed!

Winter's chill
Forgotten rains
Belatedly
Stirred long-parched plains,
Transfigured now,
Through desert spells,
By myriads
Of clustered bells.

This year, a promise
Long entombed
Knew swift release.
The yuccas bloomed!

—Ethel Jacobson

A Day's Work

A man came here today,
A cheerful man,
And in ten minutes' time
Cut down a tree.
A whirring blade
Disturbed the neighbors' peace a little;
Then the only tree we had
That you could climb
Lay stacked for firewood.

When he had gone,
We knelt beside the violated stump
And counted circles,
One for every year.
We counted twenty-five.

Oh, little ones,
Remember,
When as many years
Have passed again,
How easily,
How casually destroyed can be
One generation's loving
Creativity.

—Margaret Rampton Munk

The Tree Comes Down

Up our St. Mary's Drive yesterday they started
first with saws snarling among limbs
no doubt where nerve endings whine
and quiver.

A storm, I thought, first time
driving by the tree. One big wind
could bring it down. Likely sawed up
before it falls on someone. But rotten?
Mean spirited? We'd watched it grow.

Two hours later, I walked to it. Sawed
and split for being gathered up.
Sectioned on the ground it looks sweet
and sound throughout. Some error
by the surgeon. How much of sun and shower
dismantled in a morning and let down
out of itself a finger, a gold band at a time?

Anyhow, there it isn't, on the ground.
Maybe by spring, grass seed or baby crops sown
over the grave, lettuce, parsley, chives?
But by this evening what a confusion of shadows
and bewilderment of birds.

—Emma Lou Thayne

Summertime

In our book there's a space for a summer poem:
With what luscious things shall we fill it?
With water for splashers
And ice cream on dashers
And root beer so high that you'll spill it!

I'm glad there's a space for a summer poem,
Though I'm sure that we'll soon run it over
With bikes right for racing
And frisbees for chasing
And picnics spread out in the clover.
Now pile the space higher,
Add a tent, add a fire—
And drowsy-eyed papas and mamas,
Who chauffeur their crew
To a drive-in or two
Before we need winter pajamas.

—Kathryn R. Ashworth

Summer Shower

Raindrops
Are silver words
Speaking from the high skies
Of heaven, fragile links of love
To earth.

—Vesta Nickerson Fairbairn

Remembered Summer

The summer mountains,
Waterfalls,
Splashing fountains
In the rocky brook,
Deep pools, sun-bright,
The pines in tall
Green silhouettes
Against blue space
Of infinite sky,
The soft caress
Of whispering wind,
Bird song and flight—
This loveliness
Returns to mind,
Evoked now by
This single treasure
Of a blue jay feather
Marking my place
In the winter book.

—Vesta Nickerson Fairbairn

Costly Harvest

Sweet peas like jade beads bounce into the bowl,
Guarded close against theft before freezing.
Bottled cherries glow like rubies in the cellar,
Set among quarts of amber apricots.
I blanch broccoli and beans into emeralds
Then freeze them in cellophane-wrapped ingots.
Pine shelves bend slightly under weight of gold:
Peach bullion, corn nuggets, carrot coins.
Pints of tomato sauce bejewel my vault,
And purple beets gather momentary light
As I check opaline sauerkraut fermenting under glass.
My kitchen sends clouds of incense out open windows:
Vinegar, bay, turmeric, nutmeg, allspice, and dill
For jadite pickles, sweet and sour.
Mustard pickles gleam topaz beside zucchini relish.
Pressure processed and pristine, pureed pumpkin
Bumps crystal shoulders with jet jars of grape juice.
Tapping the gold crown of each raspberry-
    rhubarb gem,
I set it between diadems of peach chutney and
    Potawatomi jelly.
The mellow odor of drying prunes follows
    the fragrance
Of peaches and pears from the dryer.
    With miserly gloat
I sift and turn dried apricot doubloons.

I carpet the driveway deep with curing potatoes
and bulge burlap bags with carrots and onions.
Troves of red and gold apples not sauced or sliced
Dehydrate to precious chips of ivory
Or are buried in chests secure against frost.
I add up my columns of banked sunshine on deposit
And inventory diamonds crowded into the freezer.
Envy me, Aladdin, my treasure!
I sold all I had to obtain these full coffers.
And now I need winter
Lest a sudden audit catch me
With mind, heart, and soul
Empty.

—Penny Allen

Loath to Leave

The fragrance clings to the fading rose
Till the petals wither away;
And memory lingers still in the heart
Long after a joy-filled day.

—Maude O. Cook

Late September

This day is tangy sweet with ripening fruit,
Shade-cool, but blazing hot in open sun.
Such tawny autumn colors, glowing warm,
Hold all of summer's loveliness, as one
Arrayed in beauty flings her charms about
Or scents the ditchbank, field, and streams.
Late roses vie with apples, red and gold,
To rouse nostalgic thoughts. It often seems
Through winter cold and snow, let us remember,
This time of dreams and warmth in late September.

—Gladys Hesser Burnham

Drought

Have you seen a billowed wheat field die
And wither slowly with the heads still green
Until the curled leaves clatter in the wind
And all the unripe seeds in furrows lie?

Or the short grass all aquiver in the sun
In waves along a hillside arid brown
Where some hot sickle from the burnished sky
Moves and mows the blades down one by one?

So it was this year with our homestead land.
No sound of water rippled from the rocks
Or made a rim of silver in the rows
Where stems long dead lay drifted by the sand.

I grew to be as withered as the field
And hollow like the dry and wrinkled fruit,
Beholding the desert that leered untamed
After its ancient way and gave no yield.

I should have been patient beyond all fear.
For now this autumn day the clouds roll down
To lash my eager upturned face with storm.
For me the earth shall bloom another year.

Oh long upon my soul the seering drought has lain
But now I stand renewed before the miracle of rain.

—Vesta P. Crawford

First Frost

The nip
That crimps the vine
And curls the leaves of quaking aspen
Taints the shimmering
Emerald fields.
Gone are languid days
Of sun-sponged idleness
And water frivolity.
Yet now
The nip of first frost
Tweaks the cheeks of apples
And opens pinion cones
To sprinkle pine nuts
On the ground.
The honk
Of geese on marshy ponds,
The acrid smell of wood smoke
Seals summer in time.
And beckons
A new season.

—Wilma M. Rich

No Voice for This

Lonely are the ways of winter
Fathomed deep in snow;
Lonely the draped trees,
Lonely the field and stubble row;

And this I understand—I know—
I have been voiceless as the winter day
With a weight of silence on me
And nothing left to say.

—Vesta P. Crawford

Icicles

Pendant
Diamonds are these—
Loveliest wedding of
Winter and water, in perfect
Beauty.

—Vesta Nickerson Fairbairn

Profiles in Valor

Within all life
a spark of courage throbs
which bids fight back,
fight on, fight through . . . .

A silvered salmon
flails its way upstream
against the lash of waterfall
the surge of river flow . . . .

A lone tree spires itself
against the sky
from the no-soil wilderness of rock
in brave defiance to the wind
and rain . . . .

Foot-crumpled blades of grass
spring back, resilient,
and a single, fragile flower,
rooted in faith,
proves it can cleave its way
through granite
to the sun.

—Kathryn Kay

From the Sea to the Shell

The two-minded sea
Advances, retreats
Breaks on shore to run whole again.
Mollusks in the shifting green hammock
Sway in currents that fling them
Against rock
Opening a way for escape.

Empty periwinkle and moon shell,
Empty scallop and cowry
Tumble in the lottery of water
Rolled to the beach,
Holding only an echo of life
Given
And taken
By the sea.

—Bernice Ames

Unsaid Words

There is no song that larks can sing,
No perfume roses shed,
That takes the place within our lives
Of loving words, unsaid.

—Zara Sabin

Ninja

Ninja her name.
Secret-agent in Japanese.
this long-limbed black cat,
the petted resident of our house.
Walker of piano-keys,
Fisher in the gold-fish bowl.
The Youngest hugs her to his knees
and strokes with gentle touch
her midnight soul.

Ninja her name.
(Secret-agent in Japanese.)
She can hear the refrigerator door
from down the hall,
the car arriving home from school,
and be there on the stairs
yawning off her nap.
The children chatter over her
and squabble as to turns
at lavishing school news
in her indifferent ear.

Ninja.
Study in feline dignity.
Carbon-copy of Egyptian sphinx.
Skittery, kittenish, tomboy cat
grown soft and lazy, winter-fat.
Ninja with the yellow eyes
tolerating childish sighs
with purred reply.

What if Ninja dies?
I'm asked, without preamble
between the T.V. children's show
and the phone's mad jangle.
What if Ninja dies?
Will she still remember me?
Will she get to heaven?
I am caught unawares—
yet parent-wise, I realize
a small child's fears.

Hey, are you kidding me?
I gently reply.
You know the Lord loves cats
as well as kids.
"All things good," that's what He said.
Oh boy!
Then He loves Ninja, too,
because she's good.

Like me! he thinks to add,
and smiles an understanding sigh.
Ninja merely winks her yellow eye.

—Vernice Wineera Pere

21

Morning Worship

I walk from the shadows into the morning,
Pulled by your anxious hand,
Torn from the pressing weight of my hours
By your entreating demand.

We walk for a while with your hand in mine,
But I am too slow for you,
You flit ahead of me, graceful and golden,
With your own bright things to do.

I linger. How warm, how sweet the sun is,
Touching my tired face,
The brush of green ferns against the tree bark,
How lovely it is to trace.

I'd forgotten the world held such beauty,
In working, in giving my days
To the serious task of raising children,
My heart has forgotten to praise!

—Susan Evans McCloud

Seasons

It is past.
This growing season is past.
How sorry I am to see
Frost
Upon my unfinished goals and dreams.
I cast my eyes upon the harvest.
It is good
But not complete.
Yet this must be my offering.

How cold the winter is.
How silent!
Yet the snow is vibrant with
Dormant dreams.

It is ahead.
The sun is radiant
And bids me
Open up my heart and
Listen to the Gardener who knows me best.
Take the seeds He gives me.
Trust His time to plant.

—LaRene Gaunt

Appreciation
for
Self

"We love the children of God, when we love God"
—1 John 5:2

Reflection

They come not often, hours like these,
Wherein my life lies bare to me;
Wherein I see, unmasked, unrobed,
Alone, apart from changeful scenes,
Myself. In panorama pass
Chances misused, or unapplied;
Hours all unsown with deed of good,
Or that still thought which, reaching deep,
Finds, far below, some root of truth;
Wherein, as in a mirror clear,
Myself seems nothing, poor in that
The mind doth yield if tended will.

—Eliza R. Snow

Night Life

"You are courageous,"
People tell me,
"You are brave and valiant, too."
Which, though vastly complimentary
Is not absolutely true,
For I think perhaps my pillow
Knows me better than most folk . . .
It thinks me more a weeping willow
Than a sturdy oak!

—Kathryn Kay

For Example

What else is there to do
except stop crying,
regird myself, with faith restrengthening—
what's life itself except continued trying?
For instance, look at winter . . . look at spring!

—Kathryn Kay

You Heal

One morning you wake
and everything works
and almost nothing hurts.
After seven months
and the surgery up through
your mouth, screwed to metal plates
scars invisible, you even can focus.

After things happen
you heal. It takes its jagged course
upward and then
believe it or not,
so much for it,
and it is done
the chance of happening.

Then the heart of not
figuring a way back
just happens again
in the still world
like rain running the
skies and green becoming
the hand of the sun
with God standing by.

—Emma Lou Thayne

Simon Peter

You, too, rose again

As he faced his executioners alone,
The Galilean fisher in you took command
And ran,
Denying thrice
That you had dared to glimpse
A vision of celestial things.

You envied then, perhaps,
That other who,
His dark act done,
Lay dead by his own silver-grasping hand.

Your Lord met death,
But yours was bitterer
And darker.
He,
Triumphant over fear,
Self-doubt and weakness;
You,
Succumbing to them all,
Left utterly bereft—
Your Master gone,
And gone with him
The man you might have been.

In such a tomb
You passed those three dead days.

But surely as the angel's hand
Dislodged the stone,
And Mary wept for joy,

As Thomas touched the wounded side
And three companions walked together
Toward Emmaeus,

You saw the promise of another life,
Cast off the shroud,
And walked the road that led you
To Jerusalem at Pentecost,
The lame man at the temple gate,
Cornelius' forbidden dwelling,
And finally, they say,
The cross you found was lighter
Than a weighted soul.

In my life also,
May each death have
Its Easter morning.

—Margaret Rampton Munk

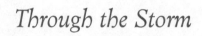

Through the Storm

"O, winter, wilt thou never go?"
My heart kept sighing sad and low.
I thought of that home far away,
Where loved ones waited, day by day,
For tidings that my willing feet
Were coming, coming, true and fleet.

Yet ever, while mine eager eyes,
Appealing, searched the heavenly skies,
Fell down the softly whispering snow,
So fair, yet sternly answering "no!"
No gleam of blue shone overhead,
But falling flakes and sky of lead.

While still the spring days came and went,
And I imprisoned, ill-content,
Beside my casement watched the snow,
Heart-hungry, sighing still to go,
Gleaming no hope from out the skies,
A lark's song, sweet and clear, did rise!

No plaintive note, but glad and high,
As e'er in sunshine filled the sky.
I could not see the bonny bird,
But still the promise sweet I heard
(Though yet the flakes fell thick and fast),
"Winter is broken, o'er at last."

Since then, though trials 'round me close,
My heart the sweet remembrance holds.
Though I the end may not discern,
My soul in trust to Him doth turn
Who token sent, my heart to warm,
Of light and joy above the storm.

—Augusta Joyce Crocheron

Shining Aftermath

In much the way
a rainbow follows rain,
there is a shining aftermath to pain.
As dawn, dark's afterwards, lights up the skies
so inner radiance can brighten eyes.
I will not weep nor fear the winter frost,
fresh green and fragile bloom are worth the cost.
I know there is no grief which cold can bring
which will not have its epilogue of spring.

—Kathryn Kay

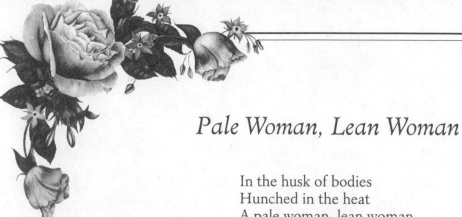

Pale Woman, Lean Woman

In the husk of bodies
Hunched in the heat
A pale woman, lean woman
Falls by his feet.

The Nazarene passes
Day-weary, drawn,
Flanked by a multitude,
Sandaled and robed;

Her hand reaches out,
Blood-pumping thin,
Pale woman, lean woman
Touches his hem,

Brushes his garment
Skimming the stones,
And his spirit quickens
Her leadlike bones.

Pale woman, lean woman,
Her faith is her plea
As he asks by the roadside
"Who touched me?"

—Kathy Evans

No Longer Missing

A drooping flag
Weeps at half-mast;
Our hearts are torn
But our fears are past.

—Eleanor W. Schow

Contrasts

I used to think the fabric
Of my days should be
A web of bright and shining strands,
Unshaded, shadow-free.
But years have yielded wisdom;
I have learned, instead,
We weave the tapestry of life
With variegated thread.

—Helen M. Terry

Journal

Put the thought
In words
And the words in ink
In a page in a book
In a very private place
Like under a mattress.

A sacred process,
Wonderful as alchemy,
Is at work
Even in the dark
While you sleep,
Making something better
Than history:

Understanding.

—Carol Lynn Pearson

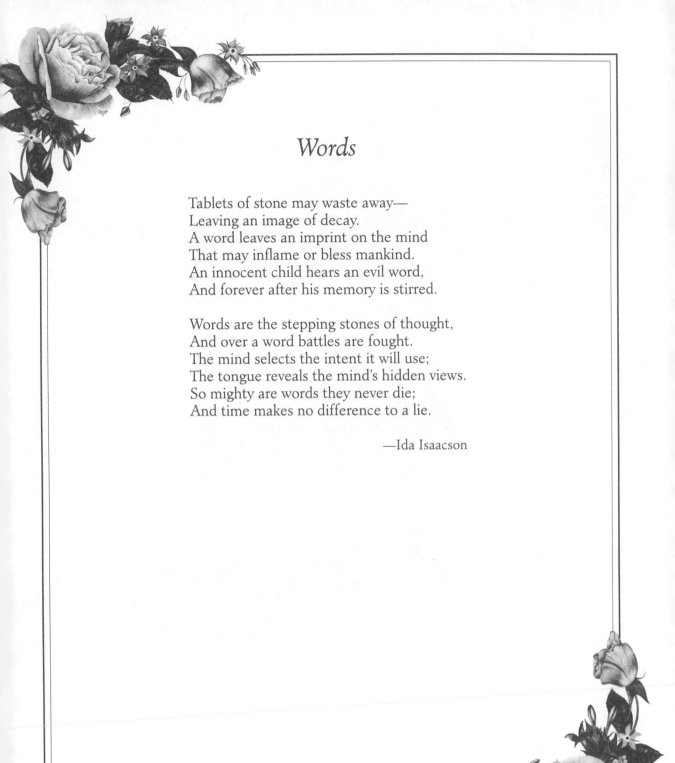

Words

Tablets of stone may waste away—
Leaving an image of decay.
A word leaves an imprint on the mind
That may inflame or bless mankind.
An innocent child hears an evil word,
And forever after his memory is stirred.

Words are the stepping stones of thought,
And over a word battles are fought.
The mind selects the intent it will use;
The tongue reveals the mind's hidden views.
So mighty are words they never die;
And time makes no difference to a lie.

—Ida Isaacson

Spirit Whisperings

How impotent, feeble and weak,
 Would frail mortality be,
How unfit to cope with the world
 And its stern reality,
Without divine inspiration
 To lead and guide us aright;
To prompt each impulse and action,
 Endow with superior light.

How futile would be all effort,
 How weak the power of speech,
How vain our bravest endeavors,
 Great aims we never could reach,
Without our Father's assistance
 To climb the wearisome hills.
To cheer, to comfort and strengthen
 Our changing, oft-flagging wills.

How poignant would be the anguish
 Found in our journey through life,
Pain, sickness, sorrow and parting.
 The cares of the world and its strife,
Without these sweet silent powers,
 Leading us into the light.
Like the fragrance of the flowers
 And breaking of day after night.

In the still haunts of the midnight,
    The silence of dawn's purple haze,
Through busy cares of the daylight,
    We list with a silent amaze
To the voices whispering to us,
    Our spirits truly commune,
A Presence seems to imbue us
    Like the joys of roseate June.

That power of infinite mercy
    Guiding all mortals on earth.
Leading through life's fitful journey,
    To the goal of Heavenly birth.
The whisperings of angels, and loved ones,
    In that fair mystic beyond,
The voice of the infinite Father,
    To whom our feelings respond.

—Eliza R. Snow

Love
for the
Lord

"Bless the Lord, . . . who crowneth thee with lovingkindness
and tender mercies"

—Psalm 103:2, 4

God

God thinks—and suns spring into shape;
He wills, and worlds disintegrate;
He loves, and souls are born.
And loving is His only way
Of bringing budded lives to bloom—
Of changing night to day.

—Isabelle Ingalese

The Gospel

The gospel is a flaxen tent
Upon the desert of the earth;
It is a purse whose contents, shared,
Retain their undiminished worth.

The gospel is a sparkling spring
Whence living waters ever flow;
A box of spikenard which has been
Prepared against the hour of woe.

The gospel is a fertile field;
White for the harvesting it lies;
And all who reap its sheaves of truth
Shall see mankind through quickened eyes.

—Iris W. Schow

First Visit of the Missionaries

The sun shone that afternoon and so did you
As I opened the door—
Truth standing there and I concerned about
    my custard
And the kitchen floor.
You spoke, memories stirred and through the
    windows, darkly,
I watched the years
And wondered what it was I longed for
And why my tears.
You went your way, but something lingered in the air,
Peace for my pain;
I picked up my mop, pretended that things could
Be the same again.

—Janet Cathery-Kutcher

Harvester: Elder Kovila from Kenya

In mundane measures he speaks
Of factory, farm, and city where
The day-to-day of life is manufactured
In plain words that speak of Here but

Ah! his narrow hands beat out
The stresses of a different weaving
In accents of lion-colored grasses
Undulating with sun and drums.

There the ebony shining faces begin
To sing, waiting in white fields.

—Mary Young

Metamorphosis

"Behold, I stand at the door and knock . . ."*

Within my faithless heart pride deafened me
Each time I knelt to pray without this door;
And choosing worldly paths, I strayed from thee,
For thy still voice was easy to ignore.
Till deep within recesses of my soul,
I heard the echoes of premortal life,
And felt despair I could not console
For time I squandered, lost in sin and strife.
How can it be that thou would come to one,
That thou consider me a soul of worth?
This wondrous thought transcends comparison
As thou art Lord of heaven and this earth.
Each day thy knock still sounds; what is my choice?
O Lord of love and peace, I hear thy voice.

—Marsha Fowers Paul

*Revelation 3:20

Born Again

As you enter the water unsinning,
I shall repent eight years
Of watching in the dark and loving
Without turning on the light.
I shall shed my old skin,
Remembering you, pink and new,
Unmarked and gifted, my gift
Undeserved.

I have served
My own unmatched desires, a rift
In God's sequence, my blue
Mondays, my bleak Sundays, all kin
To my unshriven blight.
I have loved and been unloving.
To the font I add a cup of tears.
And my own beginning.

—Mary Lythgoe Bradford

Comfort

The corner that you choose to weep in
Seems solitary, bare;
But you are not alone, my dear,
For God is near, and understands despair.

—Ida Isaacson

Light

      The lampglow
on my daughter's blonde hair
forms a halo
where she reads across the table,
the grain of oakwood between us
spiraled like galaxies and polished
to hold the light.

      To hold the light
in these late hours we have our lamps
and books. She reads from a New Testament
and I from *The Art of Rembrandt,*
his paintings have drawn me
by their use of light and shadow:
Aristotle, Christ, Jacob Blessing
the Sons of Joseph—always
the light coming from the right,
" . . . man's more sacred side."

"Man's more sacred side."
Is that what we fail as we hurl ourselves
through life? In the portraits
of Rembrandt, the light honors
what is human and what is God-like,
accepting a place where they meet,
his later biblical paintings
all completed, uncommissioned,
out of his own need.

Out of our own need,
in this Sabbath between the closing leaves
of prayer plants and the pale
blossoming of sleep, we read,
my daughter and I,
finding again the Word . . .
Light.
(John 1:1–9)

—Dixie Partridge

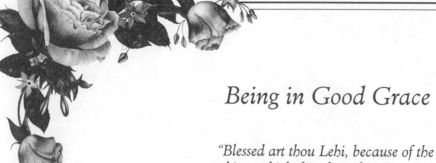

Being in Good Grace

*"Blessed art thou Lehi, because of the
things which thou hast done"**

To be seen as
acceptably clean
by One able to view
every dark strew and residue
in the structure of one
speck of dust
just doesn't
seem possible.
The miracle happens
only because of
sacred scouring
scathing all mire and
murk to bright hooray
and setting it only
clean repentance reach
away

—Dianne Dibb Forbis

*1 Nephi 2:1

Psalm for a Saturday Night

Bring forth thy Sabbath, O Lord,
    For I am ready.

I have anointed my head with jubilation
    Pressed from thy ripest blessings.
My soul has been washed in thy raining grace,
    And I am clean and shining.
O deliver thy Sabbath, for I await!

I have clothed me in a garment of repentance;
    The ragged sins of this week have I cast off.
My hair is perfumed with the unguent of forgiving:
    There remains no burr or tangle to snarl the
        sweep of love.
O sanctify thy Sabbath, and let its mantle fall
        about me!

I have adorned my hand with jewels of compassion.
    My feet are shod with eagerness for thy service.
Here in the pulsing darkness I bate my breath
    And urge the stars on in their passage.

Bring forth thy Day, O Lord,
    For thy servant waits.

—Elouise Bell

51

"This Do in Remembrance of Me"

Blinking out into the April brightness
One Sabbath after church,
I heard a Saint expound to a politely listening friend,
"With us, the sacrament is just a symbol."

"Just a symbol."
All the sunlong day and starlong night
Those slippery words shadowed me.

True enough: the bread but bread.
Yet the body offered
Up was real,
Its shattered nerves most verifiable
As pain spiked along the net.

Right enough: the water nothing more.
But the shed blood pulsed power-poor,
Streamed swift, then slow, to dry and cake
Down racked arms and flanks.

How pallid the bread when pale the memory.
Yet sweet the nourishment when we his Spirit summon
By rich remembering.

Every symbol has two halves.
But to us falls the matching.
What match we, then, in sacramental token?
What fit we to the water, and the bread?

—Elouise Bell

God Speaks to Abraham

Why
The almost-sacrifice?
Why the knife
Above your only son
While you wept?

Oh, Abraham,
I needed one
Who could understand.
There will be
Another lifted
On the hill
Of sacrifice.
And another
Father will watch,
Will weep.

But no
Merciful angel,
No man,
Oh, none
Shall stay
Death's hand
To save
My son.

—Carol Lynn Pearson

"The Bridegroom Cometh"

Zion, Thou Bride Elect:
Hasten thy purification;
Make ready for thy Bridegroom's entrance.
Turn not thine eyes on empty vanities,
Let them not feast on treasures perishable;
But with a steadfast earnestness be fixed
Upon the riches of eternity;
Let them be cleansed and strengthened to behold
The majesty and glory of the Lord.
Make clean thy lips from idle, evil speech,
Thy tongue from uttering words of foolishness.
Incline thine ear to listen and receive
Each message heralding the near approach.
Freed from all selfishness and vain desires,
Thy heart with richness then shall overflow;
So shall thy soul be filled with living light,
Leaving no room for chilling unbelief.
Wear not the worldly, ill-becoming dress,
But clothe in beauty, suited to thy state,
The garment chaste and plain to cover thee,
And peerless, spotless robe of righteousness.
From royal jewel-case, gift of thy Prince,
Adorn thy neck with gems of faith and hope;
Bracelets of honor clasp upon thine arms;
Thy girdle be of virtue, strength and love;
Sandals of speed, and courage on thy feet;
Thy hand the sceptre hold of power and peace;
Stand thou erect while over all is draped
Thy lovely mantle of pure charity.
In reverence bow thy fair and queenly head,
While on thy modest, smiling brow is set,
By Him who cometh, thy bright crown of truth.

When thou art ready, Zion, He will come
Who unmistakably declareth—"Lo,
I come quickly. I am the Lord! Amen."

—L. Lula Greene Richards

Jochebed and the Nile

She stood beside the river twice:
    At first her understanding of the plan
    could look toward the future
    as at those times, when looking south,
    she thought of waters of an endless clarity,
    as at those times her fingers,
    through the pitch, could clearly feel
    the pattern of papyrus for her son,
    child and ark the raw materials of the Pentateuch.

    The second time, while Moses
    toddled to delight the Pharaoh's child,
    there was no design except the water
    in its flood when, brown and red,
    it took the land like sorrow,
    flushing fields and rows and plains,
    its future gifts awash
    in the streaming of the moment.

—Kathryn R. Ashworth

Manna

I stretch my hand
To pluck the seed-like flakes,
Bowing over the full basket,
Feeling the weight of His love,
Knowing that from this harvest
I must grind and bake.
Small chore for sweet bread
Freely offered,
Bread mixed with tears
For this
Sustaining
Source of life.

I stretch my hand
To partake of broken bread,
Bowing over a full heart,
Feeling the weight of His pain.
Knowing that from His harvest
I may repent, take on His name.
Small chore for sweet forgiveness
Freely offered,
Forgiveness mixed with tears
For Him—for this
Sustaining
Bread of Life.

—Karma K. Wasden

Coins

Little one,
remember when I took
the five brown pennies
from your hand,
and in their place
I put a gleaming silver dime?
To my surprise,
you cried with rage—
replacing five with one
could not be fair!

I smiled, then,
at childish reckoning . . .
until I thought how often
that our Father takes away
the copper blessings
from my hand
and in their place
He puts more precious ones.
Yet, angrily, I count myself
defrauded by the gift.

I have not understood
Eternal reckoning.

—Jean Chapin Seifert

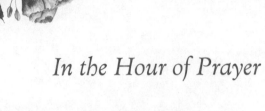

In the Hour of Prayer

In the hour of prayer
my heart gives praise
to Him who reads
the complexities of my soul
like a children's primer,
when I can only feel as
the blind man with a
beginning finger to the Braille.
And I can only marvel
how far it is from earth to heaven,
yet how close it seems when the
eye is pressed to the lens
of the Spirit.

—Susan Cole Bybee

Thankfulness
for
Heritage

"Honour thy father and thy mother"
—Exodus 20:12

Place of Prayer

One grasps more than a century
In this grove.
The trees are tall, for the years have sung ages
Behind the deep bark
And the sun has tumbled down measures of gold
Since once on a spring day
He knelt here—the Prophet boy
Soft on his knees, far from the desert
Of tongues and confusion:
      Until the truth came
      Like a spin of soft rain
To quench a fervent thirst.

Some spot of quiet sun
In each world-heart matches the gold
In this grove.
If there is peace, it spreads like a warm,
All-nourishing essence of life
From this place—
      Tall, quiet, and hovering still in the
      Sweet remembrance
Of grace.

—Marilyn McMeen Miller

Lone Woman: Charity (Arms) Everts

She must have been whip-thin to make that trek
Across the continent, her body taut
As wet rawhide, her courage ramrod stiff.
How else to leave those little graves behind,
Six of the ten she bore, one slashed to death
By peccaries, in shallow slits of earth,
That one long gash beneath a spreading oak
From one black, fatal day in Illinois
Before they reached Nauvoo to join the Saints.
Her life, her love, the husband half of her,
His body shattered by a falling tree,
To live but briefly, dying in her arms.
Through ashen, urgent lips he begged her go.
"Go with the Saints. Let nothing interfere.
To Zion, to The Kingdom—for our sakes."

Alone, with little children, yet alone,
No man to lift the heavy oxen yoke,
To grease a squeaking wheel, to take her turn
Night-herding animals, to shift the load
Of heavy boxes in the wagon bed—
To take command, to comfort her in grief
When children slipped from life. To dig their graves.
Some things I know of her, her gentle birth
Of stern New England stock, no foe to work,
For she could wash and card and spin a fleece
And weave it into cloth. She knew the dyes
Of walnut, madder root and indigo.
Her even stitch became her livelihood.

I hope her feet were cased in cowhide boots,
Her body wrapped against the elements
For I am hers three mothers down. I yearn
To see her face and listen to her words.
She made of tragedy a martyr's gift
To God, and blessings of adversity.
But more than all of these her spirit soared
Above the mud of Iowa, the endless plain,
The rivers she must ford, the mountain heights.
The clumsy, ox-drawn wagon, lit by faith
Became for her a chariot of fire.

—Alice Morrey Bailey

Sacred Ground

Sacred, gull-laden land,
With breath of mint and grass.
What shall I leave thee,
When I pass?

My footfall is so light,
Will no trace or print be found?
Tell those who follow after
That I loved this sacred ground.

—Ida Isaacson

Sesquicentennial

My people did not cross the plains.
    They walked in Brooklyn
    and Manhattan.

They were blacksmiths
    and bakers,
    drove horses,
    sailed oceans.

Their carts went to markets
    through the streets of the city
    in the bustle of downtown.
    The East was not West.

But they knew how it felt
    to leave the familiar,
    to build a new life,
    saying,
    "This is the place.
    This—
    shall be home."

They buried their children
in hand-hewn wood boxes.
Their tears wet the coffin
that shook on sore knees
in the back of a trolley
on the way to the grave.

In cold-water flats
six flights from the street,
love's warming flames
touched grandma,
then mother,
then me.

And now, decades later,
in the House of the Lord,
sweet waters of cleansing
spill down over me,
wet drops of forever.

—Barbara Elliott Snedecor

Indian Grandmother

Old One,
Forgive me for the long
Dark braids that do not
Fall down my back
And do not brush the arm
Of a fine strong husband,
As yours did.
Forgive me
For the pale words
And gray thoughts
That kept your
Good red blood
Out of my heart
For lo these long years,
These years of growing
Out of myself
And into God,
Out of despair
And into humility.
Old One,
When you find Him,
Tell Him of my love,
Tell Him I am finally
Receiving with upturned
Hands the gifts He has been
Drenching me with
Patiently,
Tenderly,
Constantly.

Tell Him how I love seeing
Your name every time I write
My own.
Tell Him I get up
Every morning
Joyous
With my heritage from Him
And my legacy from you.
Old One,
Think well of this,
Your daughter in flesh.
Speak kindly of me
When the moon begins
To bleed and He dons His
Wine-red robe.
Call me now, Old One;
Call my name
And whisper yours,
So that, hearing
Your voice, I may better
Be attuned for His.

—Charlotte Teresa Reynolds

67

A Word to the Saints Who Are Gathering

Think not, when you gather to Zion,
　　Your troubles and trials are through—
That nothing but comfort and pleasure
　　Are waiting in Zion for you.
No, no; 'tis design'd as a furnace,
　　All substance, all textures to try—
To consume all the "wood, hay, and stubble,"
　　And the gold from the dross purify.

Think not, when you gather to Zion,
　　That all will be holy and pure—
That deception and falsehood are banish'd,
　　And confidence wholly secure.
No, no; for the Lord our Redeemer
　　Has said that the tares with the wheat
Must grow, till the great day of burning
　　Shall render the harvest complete.

Think not, when you gather to Zion,
    The Saints here have nothing to do
But attend to your personal welfare,
    And always be comforting you.
No; the Saints who are faithful are doing
    What their hands find to do, with their might;
To accomplish the gath'ring of Israel,
    They are toiling by day and by night.

Think not, when you gather to Zion,
    The prize and the victory won—
Think not that the warfare is ended,
    Or the work of salvation is done.
No, no; for the great Prince of Darkness
    A tenfold exertion will make,
When he sees you approaching the fountain
    Where the truth you may freely partake.

                              —Eliza R. Snow

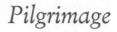

Pilgrimage

Seeing the village—
low hills and brown and bare of grass and lambs
around the clustered shops and homes and stables—
this Bethlehem, I tell myself, is where the Baby lay
    beneath a star
while angels sang the shepherds down these hills
to see the Savior.

Seeing the city—
blue and cold under the alarming cannons of
    Ramadan*
and turning gold in the morning of a December day,
labyrinth of pungent passageways and stuccoed
    dwellings
coated with centuries of smoke and dust and blood—
to Jerusalem, I remember, the Child came,
    lost in wisdom,
and the Man here scourged rabble
from his Father's holy house,
then gently healed the lame and blind ones there.

Seeing the garden—
gnarled branches on the twilight slope
where nuns sing vespers now inside a convent wall—
Gethsemane, I feel, was not in these gray,
    twisted trees:
but in his divine and breaking heart
and in the blood upon his brow—
he, kneeling here, gave all
for all he knew of what we are.

Seeing the hill—
ugly, jutting, lonely mount
where eager guides now sell their claim that this,
"This is where he died"—
I consider the power of Calvary:
I know it was for me.

Seeing the tomb—
a sepulchre at least *like* his
within a private garden place—
I imagine Mary looking up, hearing her name
and seeing—what I know by another quiet voice—
that he does live.

Seeing it all—
Jerusalem and Bethlehem,
and the stormy Galilee reflecting black and stars—
I understand:
It is by the knowing
that I see.

—Jean S. Marshall

*A Moslem holy day

Sequoia Soil or Desert Sand

I have seen saplings nurtured in Sequoia soil,
Raise their branches tall against the sky. . . .
And I have seen Ponderosa in rich mountain loam,
Grow great in stature . . . monumental high.

But I have also seen cedar on a desert waste,
Stand firm and proud despite the arid land. . . .
And pine trees clinging to a craggy granite ledge,
Grace the spot in beauty where they stand.

And so it is with man. . . . No preference is given.
It matters not his heritage nor place of birth. . . .
God gives to him whose courage braves the storms,
The gift to beautify the spot assigned to him on earth.

—Alda Larson Brown

To Shield a King

He held you in the secret of his heart,
Oh, little Bethlehem, oh, House of Bread,
And with his hugging hills set you apart,
And poured his shining promise on your head.
Here Ruth and Boaz found love's steady rock,
Here Rachel's tomb was washed with Jacob's tears;
Here clear-eyed David watched his trusting flock
And sent his sweet songs winging down the years.

Though small among earth's cities, short of street—
Where shepherds followed out their lowly ways,
And gleaners reaped the barren fields of wheat
With humble faith and peace along their days—
Obedient to his laws, you were the one
He chose to be the cradle of his Son.

—Alice Morrey Bailey

At the Well

I had come as she, the woman at the well,
Seeking only slake for the day's need,
Thirst on my tongue, my blood confused as hers
Where Israel fought Assyria in her veins,
But here I found, as she, the living fountain,
Balm for my wounds, quench for my burnings,
And my dark mirror in its quiet pool.
And here, beside this river of compassion
Have I poured out my woes and emptied grief
And let my guilt uncoil and spread my greed
Upon the sand for scrutiny, here spilled my yearnings,
Let old fears dilute, confirmed belief.
Now I am laved and full of joy and cool
As a new spring bursting from the mountain.

—Alice Morrey Bailey

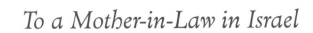

To a Mother-in-Law in Israel

There is a thought
Finely wrought
In gratitude's chamber within my heart,

That had you borne Naomi's grief
And I been Moab's daughter,
Your kindness would have drawn me thence
Where I could call you Mother.

But Israel's home
Is both our own,
Our seed of faith by One Hand sown.

So, as Rebekah, I came unto
Your tent of charity,
Where, with Sarah's tender grace,
You offered love to me.

—Alice Brady Myers

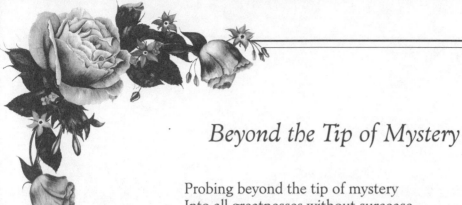

Beyond the Tip of Mystery

Probing beyond the tip of mystery
Into all greatnesses without surcease,
I stretched and bent to snatch from history,
To draw from art, a vision of true peace.

I searched wars, treaties, wars again,
The heights and fathoms of life's temporal flood,
But found no quiet thing: the hands of men
Shook with the restlessness of flesh and blood.

Till from a wandering stream arose the sweet
Of peace, and from the furrows of a plow,
And from the eager flowing of grown wheat
And gentle blowing of a blossomed bough.

In all the rich intangibles of home
Was peace that penetrated to my soul:
I marvel that a thing so great is but
The nectar from the common and the small.

—Florence Boutwell

Retrospect

No one saw the moonlight
Tangled in the myriad blossoms.
Or heard the wind singing in the night.
No one knew the tree I planted
Still dropped petals on the lawn,
Nor heard the muted voices saying,
"All are gone."

No one listened to my footsteps
As in memory I walked alone,
Back into the yesterdays
Of my childhood home.

—Annie Atkin Tanner

Wind Valley

The wind blew in my valley,
The always, everlasting wind.
Rabbits scooted through its sand drive
For the shelter of gray cedar bark.
A coyote sent his lonely cry upon its crest.
A hawk sailed its up current
And swooped in its down draft.
Red sand was hurled against raw earth;
And cedars clawed beneath the rock
For gust lashed rain.

Wind's minor cadence sang my lullaby.
Wind waited for the child, outside the
      schoolroom door,
And swept him, racing, down the street.
Youth turned his face and strode into wind's blast.
Wind whispered in the place where lovers meet.
Wind howled around the cabin of the man and wife
And the young babe.

It flung its grit into your teeth,
And blasted new-sown crops
And scoured the sky
And winnowed souls,
And knifed through sham and pomp,
And bade man send his roots down deep—
Or die!

A still small voice spoke underneath the whirl;
The night wind bore a soul back to its God
And keened the funeral hymn.

I am sick for red sand
Blown against raw earth.
I must turn home.

—Lenora Hansen

Home

Home was morning-glory,
A brook, a buttercup
And overhead a star at night,
Whenever my eyes looked up;

A promise never broken,
Like a rainbow in the sky;
The scent of sun-dried linen
And someone standing by.

Sturdy as a temple,
Unchanging as the sun,
Home was manna, and Canaan
When wilderness was done.

—Dorothy J. Roberts

Arid Theme

I speak out of the desert,
Out of the black gullies,
Out of the silence and shadow.

Kin unto the anchored sage,
With the yucca shaft I am one
Companioned by the gusty winds
And branded by the sun.

The Rain Makers Are Gone . . .

No one has ever loved the rain as I love it,
Silver waters garnered from the cloudy lands
Falling fast upon my face and laked within
    my hands.

Rain is for the bended willow trees
And fields where bladed grain is high;
Not for these unflowered hills,
These barren valleys, torn and dry.

The rain makers are gone, vapor and tool,
So seldom have I felt the rain
And yet I know that it is glistening, splashed,
    and cool.

Burying Place

> Think not that here within this hill
> The dead regret its desolate hush
> Or long for grass or budded tree;
> They who sleep beneath the brush
> Are chastened ones who never knew
> Rain within a greening garden
> Or petals falling spiked with dew.
>
> These rugged ones, born unto the arid spaces
> Have loved too long the lone and quiet places.

> —Vesta P. Crawford

For Sale

Smilingly,
She moves from room to room,
Pointing out their number,
Their arrangement
And their size.

She does not mention
That in here,
You labored all night long
On Christmas Eve
Till wood
And cloth
And paint became
A girlish dream come true;

That here you gathered
Round a February fire
For popcorn
Or for prayer;

That to this table
Many came
Hungering for more than food,
And left it filled
With family warmth and love;

That here a mother's hand,
Defying rest's insistent call,
Gave shape to beauty
With a brush or pen
While children slept;

That here your son was born.

There is more
She does not know,
And does not tell the strangers
Who have come to put a price
Upon an empty shell:

You leave the house,
But take with you
The building blocks of home.

—Margaret Rampton Munk

Buying a House

Not brick and plaster, studding, tile, and stone,
Nor floor and roof and walls—not these alone
We buy. Nor is it only land we own.

Home is the heart of all our days and nights
Where love provides security, unites
Us with the bonds of sorrows and delights.

This house becomes a sanctuary where
Togetherness enriches, where we share
Our hearthfire's warmth, our love,
    the strength of prayer.

—Vesta Nickerson Fairbairn

Afterglow

Pastoral
> Do you remember how the summer stayed; and
>   does it seem to you that it was always afternoon?
> The apple trees were bathed in amber light
>   and emerald shade that timeless June.
>
> The loaded carts reeled down the freckled lane,
>   and we would run behind them, kicking
>   velvet dust, and watch as bursting loads
>   were forked and thrust into tall stacks.
> Do you recall?
>
> The heavy-headed roses touched their lips to the
>   cool porches where we liked to pass, and
>   there were violets scattered in the grass beneath
>   the many-fingered pine and fir—
> At least, I think there were.
>
> And after, when the day was lavender, and little
>   insects played a fiddle string, and gypsy moths
>   flew round our heads on creamy wing, then do
>   you recollect how we would sing?

Pathétique
> Where are they gone—the hollyhocks we plucked
>   to fashion into dolls, the golden fruit we sucked?
> Where are the roses, once incarnadine—the fingers
>   that encircled yours and mine?
>
> Green mound, green mound, where summer rain
>   is spread, the autumn frost, the winter's
>   cumbrous snow—

Where are the occupants of the dark bed?
Is there another, near, sun-lit reality,
    where kind winds blow?

Fugue
    Do children somewhere play at hide-and-seek?
    (Those that seek me early shall find me.)
    Are there moon-lilies by a pasture gate?
    (Consider the lilies of the field how they grow;
        they toil not, neither do they spin.)
    Do tall trees write upon a roof's rough slate?
    (The boughs thereof were like the goodly cedar.)
    And are there kitchen fragrances too good
        to speak?
    (Spikenard and saffron; calamus, and cinnamon,
        with all trees of frankincense; myrrh and aloes,
        with all the chief spices.)
    Oh, sister, do you feel a gentle touch upon your
        cheek?
    (The pillars thereof of silver, the bottom thereof of gold,
        the covering of it of purple, the midst thereof being
        paved with love.)

Requiem
    When we have drawn our last, frail shattered breath,
        do you suppose that we shall see once more,
        as we walk in the creaking gate of death,
        that parlor lights shine through the afterglow?
    And will we see the shepherd coming home,
        and hear a sweet voice calling from the door?

—Virginia Maughan Kammeyer

Affection for
Family
and Friends

"Be comforted, being knit together in love"
—Colossians 2:2

Each Life That Touches Ours for Good

Each life that touches ours for good
    Reflects thine own great mercy, Lord;
Thou sendest blessings from above
    Thru words and deeds of those who love.

What greater gift dost thou bestow,
    What greater goodness can we know
Than Christ-like friends, whose gentle ways
    Strengthen our faith, enrich our days.

When such a friend from us departs,
    We hold forever in our hearts
A sweet and hallowed memory,
    Bringing us nearer, Lord, to thee.

For worthy friends whose lives proclaim
    Devotion to the Savior's name,
Who bless our days with peace and love,
    We praise thy goodness, Lord above.

—Karen Lynn Davidson

For Those Who Never Know

Perhaps her name was Sarah,
Bunching skirts up
As she turned away
From cultivated fields
To load the tools of planting,
Squinting at the hot horizon
Through a wagon's dust,
Wiping on a muslin sleeve
The sweat of prairie-tending;
Muscles,
Bending-tired,
Aching from the births of children
And of land.
In cresting waves
Long past the breaking
Of her camp,
The hoped-for green
Without her knowing
Grew.
And those of us who came behind
Found feasts within the furrows
That she left
And left
And left.

—Lynette K. Allen

Two Mothers

I am a-weary weeping so,
    My heart throbs with its pain,
I close my eyes to ease my woe,
    And see it all again,
My slain—the Crucified—my Son,
    There hanging on the tree!
'Twas not for wrong that he had done—
    E'en then he thought of me.
That other mother, coming near—
    Within her eyes there burns
A quenchless fire—a with'ring fear,
    That ev'ry solace spurns.
I pity her—have anger none,
    But O, so much of joy,
For love divine gave me a Son—
    A Judas was her boy.
"O pity, Mary, hear me, hear!"
    Prone on the earth she lies,
For grief so deep there is no tear
    To lave the burning eyes.
But Mother Mary lifts her up,
    And soothes her with caress,
Adds sweetness to her bitter cup,
    And makes her own pain less.

—Lydia B. Alder

Giving

I love giving blood.
Sometimes I walk in
Off the street
When no one has even asked
And roll up my sleeve.

I love lying on the table
Watching my blood flow
Through the scarlet tube
To fill the little bag
That bears no address.

I love the mystery
Of its destination.
It runs as easily
To child or woman or man,
Black or white,
Californian or Asian,
Methodist, Mormon,
Moslem or Jew.

Rain does too.
Rivers do.
I think God does.
We do not.

Our suspicious egos clot
On the journey
From "Us" to "Them."

So I give blood
To practice flowing,
Never knowing
Where it's going.
And glad.

—Carol Lynn Pearson

Soothing Waters

As you reach out to me
in sisterly concern,
and minister
to the mountains
of my daily living,
I marvel how it is
that I deserve
such loving aid—
I do not remember
casting bread.

—H. Joan Owen

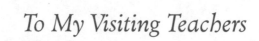

To My Visiting Teachers

I'm glad you came, my friends.
Today was not a day marked on my calendar
in red—or black.
It was just a day.
Until you came.

You came to me
and I was all I had for you to see.
My props and backdrops, even my
    supporting actors
were somehow unimportant on the scene:

Just you. Just me. We three
in good companionship.

Or maybe, yes, I'm sure, there was another
who talked and laughed and felt with us.

Because, here now, behind the door
that I just closed
as you two touched my arm and said
you'd come again

the day is new
and I'm not alone at all.

                              —Emma Lou Thayne

Good Neighbor

She did an act of kindness,
In an almost carefree way,
But it made such a difference
As I labored through the day;
My thoughts were optimistic,
My deeds reflected caring.

Oh, the joy that someone starts
Who takes the time for caring.

—Ruth G. Rothe

Leavened

You settled in my life
Like a yeast
And rose and rose
And keep on rising.

Nothing has been
So strangely alive before.
Daily I am leavened
More.

—Carol Lynn Pearson

Family Tones

When my sisters and I once
Shrieked at the injustice
Of one wearing what another
Had ironed, when we still
Exploded about the empty,
Communal shampoo bottle late
Saturday, when we snarled
About whose turn it was to
Wash dishes and bellowed
Over a locked bathroom
Door moments before a date,
And we were enemies before
And after we were confidants,
Life was too loud for love.

Now, as we quietly untangle
The knots of sibling stress
And softly straighten those
Threads which bind us blood
To blood, as our whispers
Weave the past into pleasant
Patterns, as our soft spoken
Understanding fuses ragged
Pieces of memory, as silent
Touch mends the repeating
Pain of present tears, we
Find life knitting with each
Gentle click of days, our
Lives in even, parallel rows.

—Sally T. Taylor

On Love's Sea

This is water uncharted,
Depths untried,
And I, novice sailor,
Nearly drowned once
In previous venturing,
Possessed no Titanic illusion
To send me confident
Out of port.

Now, full sail on billowy ocean,
Like trepid mariner of Columbus' day,
I want to declare,
"There be dragons here!"
And, ignorance intact,
Reverse course.

But my unseasoned hand
Knows little of lowering sail
Or compass reading;
The sailor inept,
My naivete may be forced
To sophistication.

—Blythe D. Thatcher

Our Family

The sweet dreams of the warm evening
Brush aside the whisps of years,
And bring us close again
In arms of thought
And a touch of tears,
Remembering the bright, noisy love that filled
    our house.
The never quiet, unrelenting clang and call and song.

We were all so young and never thought
That days would pass and we would part.

Now through those dreaming years
I watch my sweet and laughing child
Holding to my finger as if it were all the world.
We'll make great fun days, you and I—
Till parting comes. And with a sigh
I watch you go to this sweet happiness
I now know—
Another singing world, full of summer leaves
And comfortable love.

The two of them held all of us, for all those years,
In that bright and seldom silent circle
Circus-like and dream-like now
But real enough to bring long letters,
And after all this time,
The words that say the love we built.

—Cheris Southwell

On Priorities

Let me lean on your love tonight;
Tomorrow's crowded moments might
Find me frantic with the need
To frost small cakes with poppy seed
For eager Scouts, to soothe the cares
Of wee ones tripped by treacherous stairs.
Perhaps, awhile, a child again,
I'll stay my aging father when
His loneliness spills over. . . . All
Day long, whatever task or call,
A sister's sorrow, a daughter's tears,
A lesson written on the Pioneers,
Whatever has priority—
Mother, daughter, wife—I'll be.
But I am a woman first, my dear,
Frayed with uncertainty and fear,
So let me lean on your love tonight;
Then tomorrow will be blessed and bright.

—Mabel Jones Gabbott

His Furrowed Acres

My father looked upon his farm that day
When summer thrust its fulness, green and dense,
In leaf and root and spear. His keen survey
From hill to river-bed, from fence to fence,
Encompassed more than ripened grain, the field
Of sun-striped corn, the lucerne's emerald square.
He saw his furrowed acres sweet with yield,
His handiwork in all things growing there.

He said no boasting word, but quiet pride
Was in the sudden straightening of his stance.
His winter-nurtured plans seemed satisfied
And met the sternest measure of his glance.
In such a way I think God must have stood
And looked upon the world and called it good.

—Alice Morrey Bailey

Today We Live

Today we live, and serve, and love
Nor of the future borrow;
And yesterday's a worn-out glove
We cannot wear tomorrow.

—Renie H. Littlewood

The Warp of a Perfect Day

When the dusk descends and the setting sun
   discloses the deeds of the day well done,
Do you still remember a task—just one,
   A task defaulted and shunned away to delete and
   despoil your perfect day?
As you close your door on the eventide, to nestle
   and drowse at your fireside,
Is there one last call you have failed to keep that
   flutters your dreams as you fall asleep?
Not the alpine summit where eagles soar, nor the
   dizzy heights of Excelsior—
It's the little tasks you postpone away that mar the
   Warp of your perfect day.

—Bertha A. Kleinman

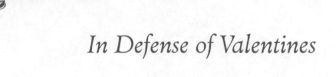

In Defense of Valentines

Now let the messages of love be spoken.
Let no one hesitate to say the word,
To send the flower, or verse, or some small token
That gives his love a voice that can be heard.

For hate is vocal. Hate sends its hurtful message
Straight to the anguished heart that must give heed;
And lust and greed are noisy and derisive—
Into the mangled air they shriek their creed.

But love speaks softly, and is often silent,
Trusting frail threads of thought too swiftly broken.
So in this day when much is mad and violent
Let love's sane messages be clearly spoken.

—Olive W. Burt

Of the Dark Seed of Joseph

Oh, world, look beneath this skin of bronze and find
    A spirit gentle as a dove.
Look deep into these eyes, soul searching,
    And find her portion of God's love.

    He who does truly mark the sparrow's fall,
    Has given of his glory to us all.

—Verna S. Carter

If It Could Be

If it could be that you and I
    Could look into the years,
And you could know my tests to be
    And I know all your tears—
I wonder, should we speed our ways,
    To heal, nor wonder how
To lay some selfish joy aside?
Or should we smile and hurry by
    And both forget, as now?

If I could look into your eyes,
    With powers to divine,
And there behold your soul's great need,
    And you could fathom mine—
I wonder, should we search our hearts
    For words of life to say,
Or should our world of narrow cares
Blot out each other from our prayers,
    And fill our every day?

O we who mean our ways so well,
    But breathe our prayers too late,
For those whose hearts beat close to ours,
    Who thirst and trust and wait—
What will the even-tide return,
    What holds its hush for me,
Whose faith is voiced for me and mine,
For you and yours, no time, no time—
    What will His answer be?

—Bertha A. Kleinman

Woman of Another World, I Am with You

For women from Botswana, The Netherlands,
New Zealand, Thailand, and Russia, talking peace

You, woman of different tongue,
awaken me.

Speak in the language of light
that flutters between us.
Open my heart to your dailiness;
give voice to your fears and celebrations
as you wonder at mine.

Your family becomes me,
the substance of what you believe
colors my view.
You take me on.

Here, here is my hand.
Filled with yours
it pulses with new hope
and a fierce longing
to let the light that guides us both
tell me where to be.

—Emma Lou Thayne

Lucy Mack Smith

As she lay there,
Two days before Christmas,
With the babe in her arms,
   The babe called Joseph
   by an ancient Joseph
   thousands of years before,
Did she marvel that the distant
Songs of carolers
Seemed a rejoicing angel choir?
Did she remember
Mary's babe?
And did her heart reach out
Across the centuries
In compassion
To the long-ago Madonna
   Unmindful of the
   shadow of the cross
   in the humble cave?
And did she hear a whisper:
"More . . . for mankind . . . save Jesus only . . ."
And feel a joyous thrill
   And a warning chill
      Of sisterhood?

—Sandra Lundquist

Understanding
of
Christmas

". . . and on earth peace, good will toward men"
—Luke 2:14

Christmases

The brown-haired doll
Is mixed in memory
With the golden one,
The tea set
With the roller skates.
The gifts you gathered
Every year
To light my Christmas morning
Have become one gift,
A pleasant haze,
Like many colored lights
All blended into white.

Small evidences, those,
Of what you really gave to me—
The feeling that I was, myself,
A priceless gift;
The gift I long so much to place
For her this year
Between the tinsel
And the newest doll.

—Margaret Rampton Munk

Christmas Eve

I change the linen on the bed
And think of him
Who had no place
To lay his head.

I trim the tree with baubles bright
And think of her
Who saw the star
Pristine and bright.

I see the tinsel's silver strings
And hear again the tale
Of glorious night,
Of ancient things.

I kneel at last on bended knee
To whisper that
I think of him
With sanctity.

—Christie Lund Coles

He was seven—Christmas was so dear.

"Do you believe in Santa Claus?"
"Well, I have—decided to - - -" (he paused,) "Believe—
For one more year."

—Elsie Carroll

A Night for Praise

This night is one for keeping faith with stars
And with all steepled hopes that rise
Skyward and far as lifting dream can rise.
It is a time of gratitude for earth—
The remnant wedge of wings that circles low
Above the drift of leaves, surrendering to frost.
The root that waits with patience under snow—
A night to shelter tenderly the peace
From secret altars where the sacrificial fires
Of our repentance burn. Unleash the tethered love
And name as blest the subtle verities of grief
That temper winds and school the heart to wear
The face of sorrow with triumphant grace.

A night to glean the heirloom sheaves of time,
Relive the parable, retrieve the singing harp.
Without this manna for our hungering,
Without the cross, compassion of his word,
Earth would be lost to all eternal purpose.

Speak grateful words that he of manger birth
Would leave celestial glories for our sake—
To meet accusing stone, the final blade.

This Christmas night sing joy in reverent phrase—
It is a night for kneeling—and for praise.

—Alberta Huish Christensen

Told by a Shepherd Boy

I followed them to Bethlehem
After the wondrous word,
After the choir of angels came,
After the song was heard.
Over the hill to Bethlehem,
Down to a stable door,
Into the yellow lantern light,
Softly across the floor,
Softly beside a manger bed,
To find the Christ child there—
How sweet his face, how small his hands,
How silky, fine, his hair.
Cradled low in a little stall,
In a place where the cattle dwell—
My heart was filled with a warming joy,
A joy no words can tell . . .
I followed them to Bethlehem,
While the stars glowed tenderly—
Now I keep my sheep on a lonely plain,
But a king could envy me.

—Sylvia Probst Young

From *Moment in Meridian*

Oh Helplessness! Oh Babe on humble hay!
Of these, the trembling shepherds kneeling here,
The Magi, traveling west to where you are,
And two earth parents looking down in love,
Who, then, could know the reaches of your word?
Could shepherds see another Shepherd, come
To lead his sheep across the pit of death?
Could studiers of stars observe your realm
Of far-flung galaxies in cosmic space,
And in their midst the majesty of God?

The lawful carpenter accepts The Son,
But does the curl of hand which grips his thumb
Foretell a yoke to bear the sins of man,
The fearful Roman use of nails and wood?
Could Mary's gaze above your petal face
See royal robes beyond the swaddling clothes:
A golden girdle, feet like fine-spun brass,
Upon an amber pavement of pure gold?
These two small feet now warming in her palm,
So soon to thread a pathway to the cross?

—Alice Morrey Bailey

For Six at Christmas-Tide

Around a table where the lamplight spreads
    A ring of warmth, a pool of golden cheer,
Sit six I love, with pencils poised, and brows
    Drawn into lines of puzzlement severe;

Of vital import is the work at hand—
    To Santa Claus they write of little schemes,
To tell him of their needs and wants and hopes,
    To ask him to remember all their dreams.

Their names are signed, and, 'ere the dream-fraught page
    Shall flutter, flame-borne, up the chimney-place,
They ask that I shall read with critic's eye;
    Anxiety is stamped on each young face.

* * *

To bed they troop, eyes full of distances—
    So many things to make them glad they see;
Their letter safely off, their prayer well-said,
    They give themselves to slumber, peacefully.

Tonight six children rest in deep repose,
    Their slates of life all clear, their troubles few;
Tomorrow they will be six women grown,
    With all the problems of the world in view.

They ask for party-dress with silken sheen;
    For necklace on a white young throat to wear;
For books and games; for fruit and candy sweet;
    A wrist-watch, and a doll with curly hair—

* * *

My eyes grow misty, and the fire-flames
    Are silver stars and arrows to my sight.
Where shall I seek to find for them the gifts
    That I would put in stockings six tonight?

I would find magic fabric for a gown
    To wrap its wearer close in happiness;
Its folds to be a cloak of modesty,
    Its silver gleam white innocence to dress.

I would find jewel of luster pure and clear—
    The thoughts and hopes of radiant maidenhood;
Its setting simple, as the purest joy
    Is found in simple task and quiet good.

Their books should whisper from the pages new
    Secrets of laughter and of hallowed tears;
Their games enchanted be—the games of life,
    And rules to play them fair throughout the years.

Where to find sweets of spirit, and of heart?
    Of kindly words to help along the way?
Where grow the fruits of years well-lived and loved?—
    These would I put in stockings six, today!

The watch should tick away throughout the hours
    And measure only moments glad and gay,
And sound a little chime when danger nears,
    And warn temptations, fraught with fear, away.

A doll I'd find endowed with power to speak
   And whisper all the joys of motherhood;
With hands to grasp the heartstrings of a girl
   And guide her into pathways light and good.

* * *

I seek in vain for magic frock and jewel;
   For witchery of time-piece, silver-chimed.
And drop, instead, a wordless little prayer
   That life will bring the gifts I cannot find.

* * *

And when their childhood days are put aside,
   May *they* dream dreams for six, at Christmas-tide!

—Elsie Talmage Brandley

How Far?

How far is it to Bethlehem,
And can I find my way
Through tinseled street, a blatant horn
And merry-maker's play,
Through the jostling, weary crowd,
The din of music played;
Past shop window's neon glare—
(The Christmas we have made!)
Past all the false and frenzied flourish
To a manger where
The Christ Child waits for us if we
But seek for him through prayer?

—Rowena Jensen Bills

116

The Star We Share

Each of us had our Bethlehem,
A mother's arms, a starfilled night,
An angels' choir singing there . . .
Beyond remembrance, beyond sight.

When we left our heavenly home,
We knew, as he, the path would be
Beset by the treachery and tears
Which followed him to Calvary.

He could mend a broken soul
As we would kiss away a tear.
We cannot do the miracles
He could do when he was here.
        Still . . . .
When Christmas is upon the land,
Faith's message is ringing clear.
The Heavenly Father, who sent his Son,
Is the same who sent us here.

—Dorothy O. Rea

Sensitivity
to
Children

"... with all the feeling of a tender parent"
—1 Nephi 8:37

Blessing

I understand it now
as I watch you walk
ascend
your pin-striped shoulders dark and
broad,
bundle of white in your arms.

The circle encloses.
Your larger hands love
lift
more than hold the sleeping child,
the word-psalm still to summon.

Father-son covenant,
humble prayer reveals
blessing
a knowledge gained not from knowing,
but from deepest listening.

Lost in dark-suited prayer,
tall father, tiny
son
I understand it clearly now.
Our separate powers are one.

—Barbara Elliott Snedecor

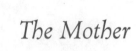

The Mother

How shall I
My love deny
To any child there is,
Since my child
Is his Father's child
And all my life is his?

Whatever place
I see his face
A glow comes in my own,
So I have smiled
On many a child
Who else would seem alone.

Any child
Is every child,
His heritage divine;
My love must run
To every one,
For every one is mine.

—Lael W. Hill

Kinship

Why?
The white-haired matriarch demanded.
Why graft this brown-skinned child
Into your family tree,
A tropic pineapple
Upon a bough of temperate pears?
Choose one at least
Who looks like you.
This one is not your son.

In pride of family,
She has forgotten
To be prouder still;
Forgotten that her family,
And mine,
Is large,
And ancient,
And of royal lineage.

She is right
That he is not my son.
He is my brother.

—Margaret Rampton Munk

On the Birth of My 11th Grandson
As American Troops Amass 8,000 Miles Away

Edward McKinley Heath, the doctor lays you on
    the draining belly of your mother
Wearied to scarcely smiling on her brutal bed.

Your robust father and I follow the nurse to your first
    cradle,
Watch the sponge, the stethoscope, the weights and
    measures.

In the ancient claim of rocking, I curl you into my
    practiced arms.
Light as butterfly wings, your hands
    flail the intrusive air.
The tart scent of your newborn head
    rushes a knowing through me
    of where you've been—
    and where I cannot let you go.

Six pounds, thirteen ounces is the nothing weight
    we all have passed through.
The joyful lightness of you I embrace in my soul
    like smoke rising from a chimney at the cabin
    or a phrase of music from your mother's violin.

You are the whisper of a night without wind,
    the comfort of an invisible map to follow.
How do I manage anything so unheavy?
    untrifling?

You now are the earth's creature,
      soon to be laden with instructions to grow by:
      this waking up—to this day, milk, then shoes,
      new rooms, a summoning to school,
      packs, suitcases, distances.

Asleep or awake, I would keep my hand
      on the small of your silken back
      to turn the strange into the familiar.
You are the tiniest person I've held.
Deep inside me, I quiver like your chin
      between cries. I lift you to my cheek, neck,
      send thin, muscular signals into our brief caress:

Grow, shine, keep being. And be anything but maybe.
To the obscene headlines of August 1990
      and to the armies of stunted persuasions
      who would make their treacherous claims on you
I send arguments fierce and quick: No.

And to you, little boy: When you are
      the weight of a man, do more than whimper
"I am only one, there is nothing I can do."

There is so much.

                         —Emma Lou Thayne

Laura

Joy lies ahead,
And pain does, too.
If I could smooth the way for you,
I would.
And that's the reason why
The foreman on this road is He,
Not I.

He did not level out
The rough terrain; instead
The Architect designed you
For what lay ahead.

That first day in my arms,
I could be sure—
God made you
Gold and steel
To shine
And to endure.

—Margaret Rampton Munk

From a Mother's Heart

I did not think these
    Hands of mine, so simply styled,
Unused to miracles and very plain,
Could ever be a source of balsam to my child
And by their gentle touch help ease the pain.
I know in life it must be each must have his share
Of pain and grief, so in my mother-heart I pray,
Let my child have the strength to bear what he
        must bear
When hurts are deeper than my hands can brush away.

—Kathryn Kay

David

A sunbeam quickly flashes through the sky
And then is gone.
The world a lighter place, the day
A brighter day.
For it was here.

A soul makes earth a visit brief
And then returns.
Pain a little sharper, awareness greater still,
And love.
For he was here.

—Udora Morris

Mothering in Nazareth

The years between his birth and his twelfth year,
Before divinity shone through the boy,
The growing time when he was close and dear,
Her little Son to love with mortal joy;

When he was taught to do the simple chore,
To hold the chisel, use the saw and plane,
To savor love behind a humble door—
These were the years that would outlive the pain.

Life's early springtime, pleasure and reward,
Each hour tender as a greening leaf.
There would come a season later for the sword,
The emptiness, the glory, and the grief.

—Eva Willes Wangsgaard

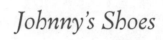

Johnny's Shoes

He read the Johnny-sized words
And I read the big ones:

"Love your enemies,
Do good to them that hate you,
And pray for them
Which despitefully use you."

He knelt for evening prayer,
Pure as Johnny is always pure:

"Heavenly Father,
Thank you for the good day
That we've had.
And please bless the person
Who stole my shoes at the
Swimming pool today that he
Won't have to steal anymore,
And that he can have more
Love inside of him. . . ."

Out the window
Or through the wall
(I wasn't quick enough to see)
Shot some small share
Of enormous wealth,
Never to be stolen,
Never to lose.

And somebody, somewhere
Instantly wore more than
Johnny's shoes.

—Carol Lynn Pearson

Opus Two

Little son,
Burnished as if by the more determined sunshine
Of the land that gave you birth—

Fashioned smooth as coral beaches
By the ocean's warmest arms,
Supple as the bending palms
Along a sunset-splendored bay—

The Artist says
He plays no favorites, but
One wonders, seeing that
He made so many of His masterworks
Like you.

—Margaret Rampton Munk

First Grief

Last night, my daughter—
Mine by right of love and law,
But not by birth—
Cried for her "other mother."

Accountable
And duly baptized she may be,
But eight is young
For grown-up grief,
The first I cannot mend
With Band-Aids,
Easy words,
Or promises.

I cannot tell her yet
How I have also cried
Sometimes at night
To one whose memory
My birth erased;
Who let me go
To other parents
Who could train and shape the soul
She had prepared,
Then hid her face from me.

—Margaret Rampton Munk

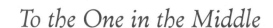
To the One in the Middle

The way will not be always silk and song
For you, my second son, the one in the middle.
Ahead the first ones freely stride along
And those behind are sheltered, being little.

But in the middle of the world are those
Whose stride is tempered, those who cannot walk
Apart, because the needs of others close
Upon them, to measure both their step and talk.

So they, like you, will learn to give and sway,
And being flexible will learn to grow,
And in the middle of the night to pray
Perhaps, and only you will come to know

The deep harmonious tuning of life's strings
That being in the middle always brings.

—Mabel Jones Gabbott

There Is in Children

There is in children an inexorable mockery.

They step with my step
to the same brittle music
played out by time.

And their pleasures multiply
(like mine).

The sun glistens on their limbs.
Even the winter longs to stay
on their sweet breath.

As their days fall like dappled dominoes
touching each other
into unsettled repose

I taste their laughter
in the tongue of my throat.

And upward, behind my eyes,
I hear the range of their voices

in tears I have held
since I could do no more
with time.

—Emma Lou Thayne

The Children

Yesterday is a big boy now—
He runs down paths I cannot see.
His laughter haunts. . . . I may not go,
But here's today to comfort me.

Today is my darling baby girl—
I hold her close in love and sorrow;
Her moment's need is mine to fill.
. . . I have not yet conceived tomorrow.

—Lael W. Hill

Children in the Night

What do children speak of in the night,
Clucking like downy chicks in the soft dark?
Telling childish secrets, cuddling close,
Watching for the first star's golden light.

What do children whisper in the night,
Near windows where leaves murmur, small birds peep,
Wrapped in the blanket of pure love and peace,
Before their prayers ascending merge with sleep?

—Christie Lund Coles

Stature

A minor scratch, a hurt, and the small disgrace
Of sudden tears is quickly gone
If a five-year-old is bandage glorified
When he emerges later on.

—Vesta Nickerson Fairbairn

Proposal

To her his words of love
Were ripples on the sea,
Or rainbows hung from sunshine's rays
When rain clouds ceased their sovereignty.

She smiled a tear away
And turned to hide another,
But squeezed a reply to the tiny voice
That asked, "Will you marry me, Mother?"

—Muriel Jenkins Heal

Solace for Tears

I have been blessed:
A child has grown
To a small, new woman,
Not mine alone,

Not mine to hold
As the child she was,
But mine to give
To a greater cause.

I have been blessed:
The child that curled
Close in my lap,
Can face the world,

Can walk alone
And can defend
And keep her faith
Until the end.

—Dorothy J. Roberts

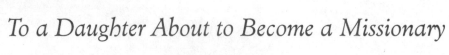

To a Daughter About to Become a Missionary

For Dinny

Twenty-two, she sleeps upstairs
between the windows of my life,
in the sleigh bed that has housed
the comings of four generations

like exotic potted plants chosen
to color bedrooms with blossoming.
Two high birdseye dressers contain her,
drawers closed on pink turtlenecks

and Speedos, walls of rackets and mustachioed
smiles. Mirrors swing her reflection
of medicated soap and squashed rollers
dropping away from night to issue

a daytime Pieta laughing and grieving,
beautifully turned out, surprising as
a crocus in snow. Other rights postponed,
the child that God intended will wear

the sanctity of the blue blazer,
skirted and frocked, innocent in her
expectation. Of course we have known
she would leave, the covers

opened and closed. It is time.
The horizon whitens. Water runs.
This is morning. She will see. France
will tell. She is changing to

the garments of The Word, will take on
the terrors of the verb To Be,
not knowing yet why departure
spells return. Five hundred forty-seven

and a half-days. She will open wide
her arms sweatered for the long cold.
The darkness will lighten and she will become
the waiting room for the willing stranger.

Kisses blow like blizzards through my empty
spaces saying, God, please. I go up to sit on
her suitcase that will not close,
press messages into her shoes,

the smell of kitchen under the leather
of her scriptures. Snow has made feathers
of trees. She lifts the sleepy shadow
of her face, steps into the air. She is gone.

I do not dare breathe in the bedroom.
Or move. Only to listen to the runners
of the sleigh bed following her.

And me unable to touch it for fear
of blanketing the sweet shiny smell
of Dr. Pepper lip gloss beneath the down,
above the furrows of knees along the floor.

—Emma Lou Thayne

To My Missionary Son

My fledgling has flown
   Half the world round—
Far out of reach of my lullaby's sound. . .
Far past the edge of a wild warning cry. . .
Far beyond sight of my hungering eye.

How can I share my warm cloak of care?
Wrap him in love in that far other where?
   Gratefully, Father, I thank thee
     For prayer.

Take on its wings the thread of my strength
And bind him secure in its infinite length.
   Let its sure pulse keep a rhythm between
   That sings of my faith in him, steady, serene.
Bring through its channels his message to me. . .
   That our hearts may be one
     In dimension with thee.

—Gay N. Blanchard

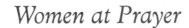

Women at Prayer

"I, the Lord, have seen the sorrow, and heard the
mourning of the daughters of my people. . . . And I will
not suffer . . . that the cries of the fair daughters . . . shall
come up unto me. . . . because of their tenderness."*

Since Mother Eve the daughters of the Lord
Have lifted hearts to Him, as her last prayer
In that lost garden, His rebuking word
Still hot—repentant, anguished, in despair—
Her first one in the lone and dreary world
Before she found the fulness of His grace,
The apple pip where future trees were stored,
The revelation in a baby's face.

And all the daughters down the centuries
Implore His miracles of gentle rain,
In thankfulness or sorrow lift their pleas
And seek to touch His garment in their pain:
Magnificats of joy or praise more mild,
But none so deep as pleadings for a child.

—Alice Morrey Bailey

*Jacob 2:31–33

Rain River

The banks are gray with morning.
Willows trail their tresses,
While darting minnows
Comb waves of blue-green water.
I watch rain kernels
Stir the river to boiling—
His river,
This crooked thing
Connecting sea and mountain.

I sat cross-legged in the place of memory,
And watched a small boy play,
Yesterday's child.
The rain was here, even then,
Chasing the retreat of pink toes,
As we ran to the cabin.
Splashing through soggy sand-beds,
We gathered rocks and fed the river.
Time wrapped us tight together,
Through the seasons
Of a thousand yesterdays.

II

Velvet banks are blue with evening.
The willows weep,
And happy waters rhythmically respond.
Another curl of fish sperm rushes past,
But the rain is quieter now.
The dream of summer is near,
And the knowledge
That you will come.

My son,
Who gathered rocks of wisdom,
To feed God's sheep on distant shores,
It will be good to see you,
Spanning the river mud,
Below the puffs of spider-clouds
That spindle the sky.
Whistling, you will wade,
As day ripples out;
Until the rain hisses
At your heels.
Then you will charge through the currents
To meet me,
And we will stand again,
Coiled into the hair of dusk,
Along the sand-bars,
Of rain river.

—Clara Laster

The Reunion

They come from miles around—
    the old, the young, the
    black-haired children with laughing faces,
    there on the wide-open Hopi land,
with few trees to shade them
    from the heat of the summer sun;
sudden gusts of wind play tag on the dusty earth,
sweeping it up into silent crescendos,
    then dancing away as quickly as they come.

I come invited from my white-man's land
    to the semi-circle of trucks, with
    tailgates hanging down like huge, flat tongues
    from gaping mouths.
I watch the young racers come across the
warm, dry land from the old place to here
    (as tradition dictates), where they
    now live in new, modern homes.
I have sat with them in their ancient kiva,
watching the purpose of life unfold
    as colorful kachinas dance to the beat
    of the old one's drum.
(Now the young ones dance in a new civic center,
to the beat of loud electric guitars.)

You, my Indian daughter, have brought me
   into your traditions,
     as long ago I brought you into mine;
we have laughed and cried together,
we have made bread together—in your outdoor oven,
   as well as in my electric one.
And again I am one with you . . .
I am the brown-skinned woman standing over
      hot stoves,
stirring thick milk gravy to be sopped up
   with fat biscuits and round, flat fry-bread,
   while yellow roasted corn and paper-thin piki
   wait to be consumed.
I watch as you teach your young children
some of my ways and some of yours,
   sweeping up silent memories
   to keep them from dancing away.

We are not of one blood, but surely of one heart . . .
the tie that binds together those who have drifted
     apart.

                 —Sherrie Ahlstrom Hundley

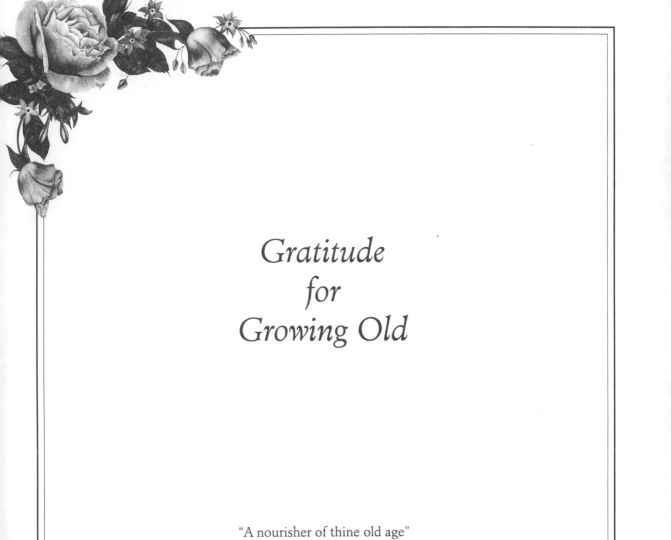

Gratitude
for
Growing Old

"A nourisher of thine old age"
—Ruth 4:15

Our former loved associates
    Have mostly passed away;
While those we knew as children
    Are crowned with locks of gray.

We saw Time's varied traces
    Were deep on every hand—
Indeed, upon the people,
    More marked than on the land.

The hands that once with firmness
    Could grasp the axe and blade,
Now move with trembling motion,
    By strength of nerve decayed.

The change in form and feature
    And furrows on the cheek
Of Time's increasing volume,
    In plain, round numbers speak.

And thus, as in a mirror's
    Reflection, we were told,
With stereotyped impressions,
    The fact of growing old.

            —Eliza R. Snow

Choice

Who walks with lowered eyes
Instead of gazing far
May find a penny, lost,
But miss the evening star.

—Vesta Nickerson Fairbairn

Blown

You have blown like feathers
Across the landscape
Of my life.

I could not gather you now
If I wanted—

You are
Too many
And too far.

—Carol Lynn Pearson

Full Measure

I cannot feel, beloved, that life has failed
To fill the promise of love's early dream:
From that far bluff, how could we two have seen
The long encumbered miles that lay between
Our dawn and dusk—the weary rainless land,
The forest standing ominous and still.
And seeing not, perhaps we asked too much
Of stubborn soil, we chafed that calloused hand
Need clear away the wood-entangled hill.

But oh, in tender memory I hold
Spring dawns that tore asunder our despair,
Piping the mountain shoulders with their gold—
And I shall also take into account
That greater thing than fruitage of the vine;
Richer than heaped-up harvests, in amount—
Our love,—which never lost its lucent gleam,
But held us to the pattern of our dream!

—Alberta Huish Christensen

The Countersign

Beloved, if oft times you miss
The tender word, the fervent kiss,
Deem not life's poetry has flown,
Or wedded love has graver grown.

Fonder than in the days we met
As lovers, do I view you yet.
Dearer as on in years we go,
Better your worth and truth I know.

No broken faith to wound the heart,
Dividing each lone path apart;
Years passing find us working still
Our walls of faith and love to build—

A temple fair and fit within
For that great Guest to enter in;
Where heart-obedience, faithful ways,
Shall count as anthems to His praise.

Then, though in silence we toil on,
Until the crown and rest are won,
Echoes from thy true heart to mine,
What none else hear, love's countersign.

—Eliza R. Snow

Spoken Late

Sharp-edged and stencil clear the moments press
Now that irrelevance is blown away.
And standing memory-deep in loneliness
I think of words that I had meant to say:
The neighbor boy returned your fishing rod,
He wanted you to know; beyond the lawn
The climbing bean is searing in the pod,
And quail that summered in our hedge are gone.

I meant to say, I know that you were right—
Love is a lantern, fragile to a breath,
Yet flame enough to light the darkest night,
Stronger than sorrow, doubt, or even death.
These words, beloved, though spoken late, will keep
The roadway clear, between me and your sleep.

—Alberta Huish Christensen

Bless My Aloneness

Bless my aloneness
As thou, too, shalt bless
The farmer sowing
In the silent fields.
Let fling in solitude's
Vast earth
The glowing seeds of hope
And work and love.
Let me behold
What challenge waits me here,
What treasure these hours are . . .
What thoughts can spring
To nugget finding roads,
Galleons of dreams returning
Filled from prow to stern
With silks and emeralds,
From lands I never thought
To know.
Bless my aloneness
As thou didst bless
The crowded years,
Help me sow roses, Lord,
Not salt of tears.

—Margery S. Stewart

Deep in the Silence

Let every man who loves entrust within
The written word a symbol of that love—
One deathless measure when its music lifts
His heart beyond the commonplace, above
All that is trite or redolent of earth—
Moon in her eyes, her profile in the sun,
How constancy of each to each resolves
In harmony of peace, two chords as one.

You lay more weight upon those lines than I—
Not yet aware that summer wind may turn,
As laughter, to a sudden chill of sound,
Leaving one broken as a winter bough;
Not knowing then how words may cushion grief
Or weave a sheath for sorrow.

Your voice calls back in penciled phrases, found
This night by chance. Priceless, this legacy—
This treasury of silent word that binds
Lost meaning to a reading by the sea,
And you, my love, to my remembering.

Deep in the silence of these syllables,
Sealed in the quiet of no sound
Against corrosive winds of time,
A new refrain is lyric now
. . . To sing us one again.

—Alberta Huish Christensen

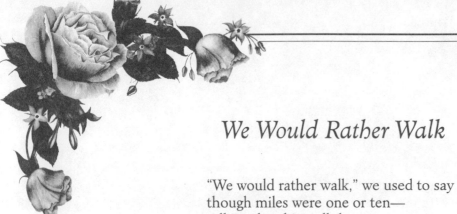

We Would Rather Walk

"We would rather walk," we used to say
though miles were one or ten—
talking, laughing all the way—
we were younger then.

"We would rather walk," we used to say
when going to the store,
"This is a perfect walking day—
walking is never a chore."

"We would rather walk," we used to say,
"it is just a block or two—
hardly more than over the way—
really kind of you."

"We would rather walk," we *used* to say—
This is springtime walking weather,
but here we sit from morn till night,
two old friends together.

—Zara Sabin

My Little Bread and Butter Life

I love my bread and butter life
Nor would I change it for another.
I'm just an average sort of wife,
An ordinary sort of mother.
I feel that fancy things are vain
Like caviar on gold-trimmed dishes,
Contentedly, I find my plain
Old bread and butter is delicious.
For me there's no monotony
Because of one-meal repetition,
And I look forward gratefully
To each meal's pleasure and nutrition.
I know that others yearn for more
And find my bread and butter meager;
But, often, all they're looking for
Leaves them somewhat more bored than eager,
And I have friends that I love dearly,
Whose lives are bread and butter, too.
We share our simple tastes and clearly
Old-hat, old-fashioned point of view.
So let those who desire their pheasant
With its accompanying strife,
Have all they want. What I find pleasant?
My little bread and butter life!

—Catherine B. Pratt

Love

Experts say that children must have
Tender loving care.
I, for one, think this is
Very true;
But some folks need reminding
Every now and then,
That middle aged and old folks
Need it too.

—Ruth G. Rothe

On Growing Old

The lengthened shadow of my life
Has fallen in contented places:
Security, no inward strife,
Dear friends, familiar faces;

Fulfillment in my family
Of hopes and dreams left unperfected;
As I grow old it seems to me
More faith and love from heaven reflected.

—Grace Barker Wilson

Faith

Faith, like a match glow
In the misty morning,
Flickers briefly
And is gone.
In mid-day its fire
Glows with the sun
In splendid brilliance
Like a field of stars.
But in the evening,
When it is the only light,
Like a lone star
On a black blanket
It is as the sun at night
The whole illumination
Of my life.

—Caroline Eyring Miner

I Do Not Walk Alone

Some say that I am going blind
Because I grope, my way to find.
They do not know; they cannot see
That there is One who walks with me.
Though the way be dark and filled with pain,
He comes to take my hand again,
For he hath said in olden days,
My child, I am with you always.

—Lucy S. Burnham

A Tapestry of Love

At first, we wove such tiny threads of hope
Pale and fragile fibers picked in haste
Flimsy on the loom, our work hung loose
Full of holes, like faded antique lace

We each had brought a pattern to create
And only shared its secrets bit by bit
Then painfully unraveled what was done
And rearranged the pieces so they fit

We chose some bolder colors, faith and work
And watched a new design begin to form
Something better than we'd either had in mind
A pattern bright and cheerful, sweet and warm

We dared claim every lovely hue our own
But soon saw need of dark as well as light
To make our art stand out in bold relief
Experience whispered even black looked right

We found a better rhythm, worked as one
Choosing basic threads both good and strong
Allowing each a preference here and there
Ignoring when the other's choice went wrong

But now, we weave in beauty as a team
Forming cloth so tight it cannot tear
Mastering the art, the loom, ourselves
Designing durable fabric that will wear

A tapestry of love we now have made
The warp and woof and weave our common goal
With faith and work and love our homespun joys
We wove ourselves together flesh and soul

—Carolyn Manning Brink

161

Grandma

"Grandma? I would not let him use that name, if I
    were you," she said.
"It makes me think of wrinkled cheeks and nodding
    gray, old head.
It makes me think of tottering feet, and eyes that time
    has dimmed,
Of wandering mind and quavering voice, and lips that
    pain has thinned.
It makes me think of gnarled, old hands, and
    shoulders bent by years;
It makes me think of winter, death; it chills me with
    vague fears."

I smiled and answered her: "I see that life has not
    been fair.
She took from you, too early, dear, a gift I hold
    most rare.
Grandma! That name brings memories of joy beyond
    mere words.
It's sweet like *love*, and *home* and *spring*, and *flowers*
    and *brooks* and *birds*.

Her feet came swiftly to my need. Her cheek was soft
   as down.
Her eyes were pools of love for me; her hair a silver
   crown.
Her hands had strength and gentleness. Her kiss could
   soothe all pain.
The refuge of her arms and lap gave peace I'd like
   again.
It makes you think of winter, death. It fills you with
   strange fears.
But when I hear him calling it I'm thrilled with ecstasy;
I pray each day for help to be a Grandma sweet as she."

—Elsie Carroll

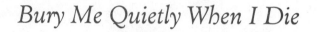

Bury Me Quietly When I Die

When my spirit ascends to the world above,
To unite with the choirs in celestial love,
Let the finger of silence control the bell,
To restrain the chime of a funeral knell:
Let no mournful strain—not a sound be heard
By which a pulse of the heart is stirred—
No note of sorrow to prompt a sigh:
Bury me quietly when I die.

I am aiming to earn a celestial crown—
To merit a heavenly, pure renown;
And, whether in grave or in tomb I'm laid—
Beneath the tall oak, or the cypress shade;
Whether at home with dear friends around,
Or in distant lands. upon stranger ground—
Under wintry clouds, or a summer sky:
Bury me quietly when I die.

What avails the parade and the splendor here,
To a legal heir to a heavenly sphere?
To heirs of salvation what is the worth,
In their perishing state, the frail things of earth?
What is death to the good, but an entrance gate
That is placed on the verge of a rich estate,
Where commissioned escorts are waiting by?
Bury me quietly when I die.

On the "iron rod" I have laid my hold;
If I keep the faith, and like Paul of old
Shall "have fought the good fight," and Christ the
    Lord
Has a crown in store with a full reward
Of the holy Priesthood in fulness rife,
With the gifts and the powers of an endless life,
And a glorious mansion for me on high:
Bury me quietly when I die.

—Eliza R. Snow

Homesick

Heaven
Light-filled, Love-filled, God-filled
I want to go
Home

—Blythe D. Thatcher

Hillside Burial

We came among the slanted shadows and the wind
To lay her there for quiet sleeping in the dark.
And when the mound was heaped with earth
　　and stones
I turned away as shaken as the brush—
To think no shrub or flower of long remembering
Might mark the arid place in years to come.
Only the seeking wind and storm of dust
To keep an everlasting tryst with her I loved.

"We got no watered land for them that's gone,"
The settlers long ago had said, husbanding
The meager stream for wheated land and garden plot.
"Why waste land that can be furrowed . . .
The dead 'aint hankering for grass or flowers."

And with dry gusts of sand upon my face,
I felt the deeper truth—the record in the dark—
Why flaunt the colored petals of a rose
As setting for this grief, or plant a tree,
Or wish for living splendor in a greening leaf?

　　　　　　　　　　　　—Vesta P. Crawford